Gather the Children

by Joshua White

Contents

1. Why Sabbath School? 5

2. The Family Bible-Study Sabbath School Model 9

3. Why Integrate All Ages? 13

4. Why Bible-Based? 25

5. "Interesting" vs. "Entertaining" 33

6. Tips for Teachers 39

7. Qualifications of Teachers 51

8. The Role of the Parents 65

9. Practical Points 71

10. Common Questions or Objections 77

11. Ready to Start! 83

12. Success Stories 85

Chapter 1

Why Sabbath School?

"The Sabbath school work is important, and all who are interested in the truth should endeavor to make it prosperous." (*Testimonies for the Church* vol. 5, 127)

We all want our Sabbath school to be interesting, engaging, and, most importantly, a tool for the salvation of our precious young people. We hope every week that the class will be interesting, that everyone will have studied and are engaged and involved. As teachers, we hope that our students are happy and excited. But more often than not, especially in youth classes, we find young people unengaged, unstudied, and very much uninterested.

How to make Sabbath school interesting and engaging for everyone has been a topic of much discussion for years in our church. We have tried many methods. But have we tried the plans of the Lord?

Many and varied are man's ideas, while God's method is simple and singular. Man often follows societal norms or tradition, while God says that His ways are not the ways of this world. Man seeks for new and fanciful ideas to achieve great things, while God's beautiful designs were instituted since the beginning, and the realization of results that will surprise the world awaits only their trusting, humble application to the modern circumstance. It is vital that we do not continue with certain methods just because it is the way it's always been. Rather, we must constantly ask, "What sayeth the Lord?" and seek to humbly follow God's ways and methods.

We are told, "The Sabbath-school, **if rightly conducted**, is one of God's great instrumentalities to bring souls to a knowledge of the truth." (*Testimonies on Sabbath-School Work*, 18, emphasis supplied)

What powerful encouragement! But, notice, the Sabbath school must be *rightly conducted*. This tells us that, while Sabbath school is vitally important, it is not enough to merely *have* Sabbath school. It must be *rightly conducted*. There is a work for us to do in shaping, planning, and conducting our Sabbath schools so that they can accomplish the purpose which God designs them to.

"The Sabbath school should be one of the greatest instrumentalities, and the most effectual, in bringing souls to Christ." (*Testimonies on Sabbath-School Work*, 20)

"Our Sabbath schools are nothing less than Bible societies, and in the sacred work of teaching the truths of God's word, they can accomplish far more than they have hitherto accomplished." (*Counsels on Sabbath School Work*, 9)

"The Sabbath school is an important branch of the missionary work, not only because it gives to young and old a knowledge of God's word, but because it awakens in them a love for its sacred truths, and a desire to study them for themselves; above all, it teaches them to regulate their lives by its holy teachings." (*Counsels on Sabbath School Work*, 10)

"The Sabbath school should be the place where, through a living connection with God, men and women, youth and children, may be so fitted up that they shall be a strength and blessing to the church." (*Counsels on Sabbath School Work, 11*)

As we fight the battle for the souls of our children and youth, we need to use every weapon in our arsenal, but we must use them intelligently. The Sabbath school and the Bible are important weapons in our arsenal, but a weapon poorly used may result in more damage to the user than to the enemy. Proper use is vital.

I praise the Lord that we do have instruction on how to properly conduct our Sabbath schools and how to properly use the Bible in this context to help reach our youth, bring up our children, interest them in the Scriptures, and help them to be spiritually strong.

This short book will help explain one way that we can have our Sabbath school *rightly conducted*. The method here explained is one that involves the entire family – all ages – and provides a context for the study and grounding of our children and youth in the Word of God. It is called the *Family Bible-Study Sabbath School.*

Chapter 2

The Family Bible-Study
Sabbath School Model

S uccess in any line demands a definite aim," we are told in the book *Education*, 262. To have success in our Sabbath-school endeavors, we need to understand our goal. To that end, let us identify four important goals for an effective Sabbath school program.

1. To motivate and encourage Sabbath school attendance

Most commonly, church has higher attendance than Sabbath school. Why? Perhaps people don't find Sabbath school interesting? Attendance will increase with interest. Sabbath school should be so interesting that people want to attend because they are learning something there.

2. To interest everyone – especially our children and youth – in the Bible

The Word of God is our only safe guide, and no other study is more important for children, youth, and adults alike. "Who of our youth can know anything of what is truth, in comparison with error, unless they are acquainted with the Scriptures?" (*Christian Education*, 113).

How can we help our children and youth learn more of the Scriptures? Interest is a vitally important motivating factor for learning. Sabbath school should be a place where we help foster a vibrant interest in the Word of God.

3. *To help guests and new believers engage in Bible study*

To fulfill the call of the great commission and demonstrate our love for souls, we must seek to help those who are searching for truth to develop habits of Bible study. It is not enough that people come to church and hear a message, nor should we merely draw their attention to the words and writings of man. They need to be interested and motivated to study the Bible for themselves. Sabbath school should provide a model of and an experience in Bible study that guests and new believers can take with them and continue in their homes.

4. *To help everyone be grounded in the fundamental truths of the Bible*

Sadly, very few people are familiar enough with their Bibles to be thoroughly grounded in the most basic fundamental doctrines. Many don't know the details of the important stories of the Bible. Why? Because we don't study them often. The Sabbath school should be a place where all can become firmly grounded in the stories, teachings, and beautiful truths of the Bible.

As a means of accomplishing these four goals, the Family Bible-Study Sabbath School model is a highly effective tool. What is the Family Bible-Study Sabbath School model? It is as simple as it sounds: the entire family, all ages, come together with other families to study the Bible. The lesson is studied throughout the week as part of family worship, and at Sabbath school all gather in a circle, reading from the Word of God, discussing, sharing lessons learned, and discovering truths new and old.

Churches following this model have experienced amazing results.

- In larger churches with many classes, the Family Bible-Study Sabbath School is usually the most well-attended class. In smaller churches, the entire church enjoys uniting in the experience and finds relief from the often sparsely-attended, age-segregated model with its inherent difficulties of organization common to a small church.
- Visitors remark that the Family Bible-Study Sabbath School is the best Sabbath school they have ever attended.
- Sabbath school attendance increases dramatically.
- Previously uninterested and uninvolved young people begin taking an active part in the Sabbath school class and become interested in studying their Bibles.
- Children, with their families, become conversant in their Bibles.

Two vital components are essential to realize the potential of this model – 1) age integration, and 2) Bible study. The method will not be as effective as possible without both of these factors combined.

Traditional Sabbath school environments are age-segregated, placing young children with young children, older children with older children, teens with teens, and adults with adults. Sometimes even the adults are separated into young adult and older adult classes. The Family Bible-Study Sabbath School is based, as its name suggests, in the family, and is thus a mixture of *all* ages – children, youth, and adults. Everyone, from the oldest to the youngest, comes together in the same class. As we will see later, this is Biblical principle and has many benefits besides.

However, while integrating all ages is a very important factor, this alone is not sufficient without proper structure and methods. There are many family or age-integrated Sabbath school programs in use among churches of many denominations today, but not all are effective in fulfilling God's design for Sabbath school. Here lies the value and importance of the second component – *Bible study.*

You may be asking, how do we combine all ages and still keep the interest of all? How can the old and the young study the same lesson? God's word has a power to instruct all ages which we do not fully understand. The teachings of Jesus were simple enough for a child to understand and yet they challenged the greatest minds of His day. This should not surprise us. After all, God is the creator of the human mind and has the power to meet the needs of young and old alike through His Word.

Some Sabbath school programs – even some family-integrated ones – focus more on keeping the children entertained than on involving them in the study of the Bible. This often results in making adults rather bored throughout the class and not effecting lasting interest in God's word for everyone. Other Sabbath school programs use a man-made lesson with very little real Bible study, thus not tapping into this amazing source of age-integrated instruction.

The Sabbath school model we will consider here is one that *simply takes the Word of God, without depending on entertainment* or *upon the writings of man, and makes that Word the basis of all study.* The most effective Sabbath school model is one which beautifully combines the components of age integration and Bible study – thus the Family Bible-Study Sabbath School.

Let us discuss these two core components – "family", or age integration, and "Bible-Study" – in greater detail in the following chapters.

Chapter 3

Why Integrate All Ages?

There are several reasons why the concept of age integration is beneficial to both children and adults. We will consider a few of them here.

1. Age integration is supported by science.

From a purely secular standpoint, scientific research has made it clear to us that the method so common today in which children spend the majority of their time with other children approximately the same age, throughout their schooling and in their recreation and sports, is not the most beneficial option for children, youth, or adults. In fact, nearly the only evidence we can find for its favor is the mere fact that it is commonly done – so common that we assume it's good. This fact, of course, holds little weight in support of the idea, and to further undermine its validity, it has only been normal for a rather short period of time in earth's history.

The idea of age segregation en masse originated when schooling began en masse.

"The placement of children in separate classes with others of the same age is a fairly recent phenomenon. Age segregation did not occur in full force until the advent of compulsory education laws brought a large influx of children to the public school system." (Jay Fieldman and Peter Gray "Some educational benefits of freely chosen age mixing among children and adolescents" *Phi Delta Kappan* 80, no 7, (1999), 507-512)

On a global scale, the concept of age segregation is only about 150 years old. Age segregation was the logical result of compulsory education. Yet this setting is not natural in real life. Children have learned in the context of the family, or at least within a wide range of ages, throughout history.

"Never in history until the 20th century have young people been largely separated from the ongoing productive activities of society." (Gunhild O. Hagestad and Peter Uhlenberg, "The Social Separation of Old and Young: A Root of Ageism" *Journal of Social Issues* 61, no 2, (2005), 343-360)

The scientific research is clear that the best environment for learning, even in secular school, is not an age-segregated one. Learning occurs best in an age-integrated environment. Developmental and educational psychology have shown us that children develop best by working together with more competent individuals, rather than being segregated into groups of similar ability and age. Studies have found that age-mixed students perform better academically than do their single-age classroom counterparts. Educators report advantages in the areas of academics, self-esteem, and socialization skills in an age-integrated environment. Studies in age-integrated schools in which older students are helping younger ones have shown greater maturity and thinking abilities in all ages – better in the young ones because they are looking up to older role-models, and better in the older ones because they are figuring out methods for teaching the younger children.

Even socialization abilities are improved by the age-integrated environment. Researcher Dr. Larry Shyers points out, "The results seem to show that a child's social development depends *more on adult contact* and less on contact with other children as previously thought." Numerous other studies have found *improved* socialization skills in children and young people growing up in an age-mixed environment.

Of course, this is no surprise to God, for, "In His wisdom the Lord has decreed that the family shall be the greatest of all educational agencies." (*The Adventist Home*, 182) God ordained for the family – which is inherently age integrated – as the original and ideal learning environment.

Compulsory education broke a longstanding tradition of learning within a wide range of ages by instituting this concept of age-segregation, and science now is showing us that this was a mistake. Let us not make the same mistake by structuring our Sabbath schools based on this man-made invention.

2. Age integration is a Biblical model.

In addition to the lack of scientific support for age-segregation, we find no precedent in Scripture for an age-segregated educational environment. This fact, of course, should hold much greater weight with us than the science and research of man, as interesting and helpful as that science may be. *The Bible does not give us either instruction or example of age-segregated environments for education or spiritual instruction.* In fact, it gives us the opposite. Repeatedly there is specific instruction to include the children during spiritual gatherings.

"Gather the people together, **men** and **women**, and **children**, and thy **stranger** that is within thy gates, that they may hear, and that they may learn, and fear the

LORD your God, and observe to do all the words of this law: and that their children, which have not known any thing, may hear, and learn to fear the LORD your God, as long as ye live in the land whither ye go over Jordan to possess it." (Deuteronomy 31:12,13)

"There was not a word of all that Moses commanded, which Joshua read not before **all the congregation** of Israel, with the **women**, and **the little ones**, and the **strangers** that were conversant among them." (Joshua 8:35)

"And **all Judah** stood before the LORD, with their **little ones**, their **wives**, and their **children**." (2 Chronicles 20:13)

"Now when Ezra had prayed, and when he had confessed, weeping and casting himself down before the house of God, there assembled unto him out of Israel a very great congregation of **men** and **women** and **children**." (Ezra 10:1)

"Gather the people, sanctify the congregation, assemble the **elders**, gather the **children**, and **those that suck the breasts**: let the bridegroom go forth of his chamber, and the bride out of her closet." (Joel 2:16)

Throughout the history of God's people, when they came together to learn God's word they did not separate according to age. They learned together *as a family*.

Why do we find age segregation as the norm for Sabbath schools? Sadly, it is for the same reason that it is the norm in academic learning environments. It is the plan of our enemy to separate children from those of a more mature mindset. He wants to prevent their opportunity to learn how to relate to others of varying abilities, backgrounds, ways of thinking, and ages and to normalize everyone to be like everyone else instead of rising to spiritual maturity and strength as modern Daniels.

The scientific research is clear that age integration is the best environment for learning, and the Word of God is clear that this is the method He has given His people. Family-integrated Bible study is the Biblical model.

3. Age integration helps build a bond between parents and children.

Satan is constantly seeking to separate the beautiful family unit which God has created. Age-integrated classes strengthen the family unit by having all the members of the family study the same topic and material. Instead of the young children studying one Sabbath school lesson, older children studying another lesson, teens studying another one, and adults studying yet another lesson, the parents and children are studying the *same* lesson together – not only on Sabbath, but throughout the week.

This places everyone in the family "on the same page," provides valuable ingredients for interactive and engaging conversations throughout the week, and helps build a bond between parents, children, and siblings. Instead of parents dropping off their children at their class on Sabbath morning, the parents and children go to class together, learn together, and share the same experiences and discussions together. This is a bonding experience which strengthens those ties between parents and children which God designed should last for eternity.

4. Age integration empowers parents to disciple their children.

In the age-integrated class method, parents are better able to be involved in what their children are studying.

They are also able to relate events throughout the day and week to what they are studying, as Deuteronomy 6:6 and 7 instructs them to do.

When families are separated in the age-segregated Sabbath school model, a subtle wall is built that disconnects the members of the family, and Satan will work hard to reinforce that barrier. We are told, "Some parents do not understand their children and are not really acquainted with them. There is often a great distance between parents and children." (*The Adventist Home*, 190) The man-made divider of age-segregation promotes disharmony between ages rather than unity. Through the practice of age- segregation in church and school, parents gradually lose the ability to disciple their children, and children lose the ability to relate to their parents.

Rather than pulling families apart, the church should make every effort to strengthen the family. The age-integrated Sabbath school model educates and equips parents to teach and disciple their children instead of expecting the church to do this for them. It helps parents be better parents, supports them in their parenting role, and helps unite the family.

In addition, age-integrated Sabbath schools encourage and enable parents to follow the model set forth in Deuteronomy 6:6,7, which admonishes parents to talk about God's word with their children when they are sitting, walking, lying down, and rising up – in other words, all throughout the day. As parents and children are studying and learning the same material, relating everyday experiences to what they are studying becomes more natural.

The church should encourage parents to bind the hearts of their children to theirs. When children and parents worship, study, and learn together, hearts are drawn to one another and common bonds are formed that can spiritually strengthen both the parents and the children and thus the church.

Furthermore, when children desire to be with their parents and when the members of the household are united, it speaks volumes and piques the interest of the world. The united family, with strong parent-child relationships, is powerful evidence in favor of the truth.

"One well-ordered, well-disciplined family tells more in behalf of Christianity than all the sermons that can be preached." (*The Adventist Home*, 52)

"A well-ordered family [is] evidence of the power of the truth! When it is seen that the children are not like worldlings, when the beauty of faith and the spirit of genuine Christianity are seen in them, it will be as a light pointing heavenward." (*The Review and Herald*, May 22, 1888)

5. **Age integration nurtures cross-generational relationships.**

Age-integrated environments help children learn how to communicate with and relate to adults and help adults learn to communicate with and relate to children. Many youth struggle to speak and relate to adults for the simple fact that they have not spent much time with adults during childhood.

"How touching to see youth and old age relying one upon the other: the youth looking up to the aged for counsel and wisdom, the aged looking to the youth for help and sympathy. This is as it should be. God would have the young possess such qualification of character that they shall find delight in the friendship of the old, that they may be united in the endearing bonds of affection to those who are approaching the borders of the grave." (The Signs of the Times, October 19, 1888)

"There is blessing in the association of old and young. The young may bring sunshine into the hearts and minds of the aged. Those of hoary heads need the vitality and action of the young. And the young need the wisdom and mature experience of older persons. There is to be a blending of the two." (Spalding and Megan Collection, 258)

6. Age integration teaches consideration for others.

Age-integrated environments provide an opportunity to nurture respect, consideration for others, and social maturity. In an age-integrated environment, the older youth and adults can learn to have patience for the younger children. The younger children can also learn to listen and respect and value the input of the older generation.

Conversely, in situations of age segregation, the old often develop impatience toward the young and the young develop a lack of respect for the old.

7. Age integration builds unity in the church.

Age-segregated Sabbath schools often unintentionally create separation and non-cohesiveness among the members of the church. When the little children attend their class, the teens attend their class, and the adults attend their class, it is very easy for the Sabbath to pass without a child having a spiritual conversation with an older individual. In the family-integrated Sabbath school, four-year-olds and seventy-year-olds can share thoughts and insights on the beautiful stories of the Bible. The Family Bible-Study Sabbath School brings generations together on a deeper level than almost any other means. This sharing builds a strong unity in the church and family like nothing else can.

8. Age integration early cultivates in teens the disposition to engage spiritually.

A lack of spiritual interest is common in our youth today; yet, we often wait until this age of youth to initiate real spiritual development and deep Bible study. If we want spiritual participation and strength in the teenage years, we need to start in childhood.

If youth are accustomed to being mere receivers or to being entertained during the Sabbath schools of their childhood, it will be a challenge for them to be expected suddenly to engage in adult Sabbath school. But if they are engaged in mature spiritual activities through the Family Bible-Study Sabbath School from an early age, the "transition phase" in which a young person may feel awkward to be interested in spiritual things is removed.

The family-integrated Sabbath school provides a comfortable environment from an early age for a child to participate in and contribute to spiritual settings long before he is a teenager. If involved in meaningful spiritual activities on an age-integrated level from an early age, there is little chance that the youth will go through a stage of disinterest.

9. Age integration encourages spiritual maturity and trains and prepares children to be spiritual leaders.

It is important that we train our youth to be spiritual leaders in our churches and in their homes. Family-integrated

Sabbath schools are effective tools in accomplishing this. When children spend the first fourteen years of their lives going to a Sabbath school where they are the audience to be taught (or entertained), rather than being expected to meaningfully participate, they will struggle to transition to spiritual leadership in the church. In contrast, age-integrated environments provide children with the opportunity to make meaningful contribution to spiritual things, and even experience some aspects of leadership, from an early age. The transition to leadership in the church will be a natural one because they already have experience.

10. Age integration inspires our youth to nobler aspirations.

Young people are counseled by the Lord: "Aim high, and spare no pains to reach the standard." (*Fundamentals of Christian Education*, 82) Age segregation tends to not challenge young people to nobler aspirations: rather, it often encourages immaturity by depriving young people of adult role models. Young people learn primarily by example. How can young people grow to be spiritually mature when they are separated from those who are spiritually mature? Surrounding children and youth by those of the same age, who are generally at the same level as they are, is not the most effective method of teaching them to aim high.

"Satan works through young associates to influence and corrupt the minds of each other. **It is the most effectual way he can work**. Young associates have a powerful influence over one another. Their conversation is not always choice and elevated." (*The Review and Herald*, January 20, 1863, emphasis supplied)

"Impressions made upon the minds of the young are hard to efface. How important, then, that these impressions should be of the right sort, bending the elastic faculties of youth in the right direction." (*Testimonies to the Church* vol. 4, 198)

The influence of the association formed within age-segregated classes, and especially youth groups, is not one to be taken lightly. The lack of maturity, wisdom, and spiritual guidance from older adults negatively affects the spirituality of the youth.

On the other hand, placing them among those who are older and more experienced is a God-given method which helps them to see a higher goal and encourages them to "stretch every spiritual nerve and muscle" (*The Youth's Instructor*, July 27, 1899)

Teaching children by example and through association with adults is the pattern that the Lord gave to the Hebrews. The instruction given multiple times in Deuteronomy was for the parents to be the spiritual instructors and guides of their children. We find examples in the Scriptures of the danger of the youth relying on their companions for counsel, like the story of Rehoboam. "But he (Rehoboam) forsook the counsel of the old men, which they had given him, and consulted with the young men that were grown up with him, and which stood before him." (1 Kings 12:8)

The Lord intends for the wisdom gained through years to be passed down to the youth. For example, the prescription given in Titus 2:4-5 has older women training and discipling younger women. Proverbs 16:31 tells us, "The hoary head is a crown of glory, if it be found in the way of righteousness." Instead of separating the young and the old, we should bring them together.

"The Lord desires the younger laborers to gain wisdom, strength, and maturity by association with the aged laborers who have been spared to the cause." (*Testimonies for the Church* vol. 7, 289)

There is increased spiritual maturity among those who have the opportunity to be a part of an age- integrated environment. Young boys are more likely to grow up to be men who are strong spiritual leaders because they are surrounded by leaders instead of peers. The young feel a sense of responsibility and belonging in the church when they are contributing rather than merely receiving.

On the other hand, age-segregation tends to cultivate a passive attitude among the youth. It allows the youth to see themselves as "outsiders" and communicates to them that they cannot understand the deeper spiritual matters of the adult class and that serious spirituality is not required of someone their age. It reinforces to young people a youth subculture identity rather than a family identity, turns the hearts of the children away from their parents, and contributes to teenage rebellion.

The age-segregated concept has been given sufficient years to produce fruit. The evidence clearly shows that generational fragmentation rarely produces young people who are serious about religion or a relationship with God. It does not promote unity of the family or the church. Let us rediscover God's method for discipling our young people through the age-integrated church setting.

Chapter 4

Why Bible-Based?

The Sabbath school should be a place where the jewels of truth are searched for and rescued from their environment of error, and placed in their true setting in the framework of the gospel." (*Counsels on Sabbath School Work*, 12)

We have seen that the age-integrated family model is ideal. But the question that arises is, "How do we make the lesson applicable to all?" Let us discuss the second point of the Family Bible-Study Sabbath School – that of the class being Bible based.

There are different perceptions the meaning of "Bible-based". Some may consider a set of lessons that uses a few Bible verses to be Bible-based. Others consider a lesson Bible-based simply because they discuss a particular story or lesson from the Bible. "Bible-based" in the context of the Family Bible-Study Sabbath School means to actually use the Bible, and the stories thereof, in place of a lesson as the core of the Sabbath School.

One of the most powerful reasons for Bible-based study is that the Word of God possesses the power to transform. Scripture tells us, "The entrance of thy words giveth light; it giveth understanding unto the simple." (Psalm 119:130)

As wonderful and inspiring as lessons written by a human author may be, no lesson written by man, however good, has power to transform. Only the word of God has this power. "For the word of God is quick and powerful, and sharper than any two edged sword, piercing even to the dividing asunder of soul and spirit, and is a discerner of the thoughts and intents of the heart." (Hebrews 4:12)

"The creative energy that called the worlds into existence is in the word of God. This word imparts power; it begets life. Every command is a promise; accepted by the will, received into the soul, it brings with it the life of the Infinite One. It transforms the nature and re-creates the soul in the image of God." (*Education*, 126)

"He who with sincere and teachable spirit studies God's word, seeking to comprehend its truths, will be brought in touch with its Author; and, except by his own choice, there is no limit to the possibilities of his development." (*Education*, 124)

"Those who open their hearts to receive the truth will realize that the Word of God is the great instrument in the transformation of character." (Letters and Manuscripts 13, Manuscript 68, 1898)

"As the penetrating power of the leaven produces an entire change in the meal, so the power of the Word of God, through His grace, will work a transformation in the soul." (*The Signs of the Times*, October 27, 1898)

We want to be transformed. We want our children and youth to be transformed. With such power awaiting our use, we should make our Sabbath schools a means of helping each member tap in to this incredible, life-changing source of power! Let us use the tool which is best designed to make this transformation happen, and remember that "immeasurably superior in value to the productions of **any human author** are the Bible writings." (*Education*, 125, emphasis supplied)

Another incredible benefit of Bible study is that the Word of God is suited for *every age*. Jesus' teaching was simple enough for the little child to understand but profound enough to challenge the greatest minds of the day. This is the power of the Word of God, and it is a power that we can't quite understand. It is designed for all ages. There is no introduction in the Bible telling us to only use it after a certain age. God's Word is designed for all.

"There is light enough given in the word of God, so that none need err. The truth is so elevated as to be admired by the greatest minds, and yet it is so simple that the humblest, feeblest child of God can comprehend it, and be instructed by it." (*Testimonies for the Church* vol. 1, 338)

This is something man cannot do. When an author writes books or lessons, what is the first thing he/she considers? The age of the audience! An author will adapt the writing for children, or young people, or adults, etc. depending on his intended audience. God, the greatest of all authors and the creator of the human mind, has designed a source of instruction for all ages in one single package.

Consider the methods of teaching that Jesus used. "Christ's way of presenting truth cannot be improved upon....**The words of life were presented in such simplicity that a child could understand them**....Although the great truths uttered by our Lord were given in simple language, they were clothed with such beauty that **they interested and charmed the greatest intellects**." (*Evangelism*, 56, emphasis supplied)

Speaking of the words Jesus used in prayer, and certainly applicable to other of His words, "As one with humanity, [Jesus] presents His own ideal of prayer, words so simple that **they may be adopted by the little child, yet so comprehensive that their significance can never be fully grasped by the greatest minds**." (*Prayer*, *290*, emphasis supplied)

"How plain were Christ's words! How simple the language! A child could have understood it. But the disciples were perplexed." (*The Review and Herald*, October 19, 1897) Who was perplexed? Who was confused? Not the children. Who is the interpreter of the Word of God? It is the Holy Spirit. Is the Holy Spirit not able to speak to a child's heart? The word of God is suited for every age.

Some think that in an age-integrated Sabbath school someone must be left out. We think either the adults don't get fed because we have to use a child-adapted lesson or the children will get bored because we gear the lesson toward the adults. In the family Bible-study class, we use the one Book that contains lessons that are adapted for every age.

In light of this fact, let us be careful in our selection of Sabbath school materials to use the Word of God. While the lessons, books, and other writings of man may be helpful at times, *if we want to tap into the power-source of age-integrated teaching we must use the Word of God itself.*

We should also remember that certain parts of the Bible as better suited to all ages than others. The stories of the Bible are best, and we should seek to use these as much as possible. We are told that the stories of the Bible are especially designed to awaken the interest of the child. "In all that men have written, where can be found anything that has such a hold upon the heart, anything so well adapted to awaken the interest of the little ones, as the stories of the Bible?" (*Education*, 185)

These stories have been compared to a large pool of varying depths. In this same pool a toddler can enjoy wading, an older child can learn to swim, and an adult can do deep diving. The stories of the Bible are at the same time simple enough that even a young child can understand them and profound enough for the greatest minds to explore.

While there certainly are correct and incorrect methods of using the Bible in the Sabbath school setting (more on this later), the important point here is that if we are looking for content that is accessible, applicable, and useable by all ages, the Bible is the one and only material that fills this role.

The value of Bible study cannot be overestimated. It should take the central role in our Sabbath schools. Sabbath school teachers are counseled, "Exert every influence you can possibly command to interest them in the Scriptures." (*Sabbath-School Worker*, March 1, 1893)

There is much counsel on the importance of Bible study. Here are a few more statements from the Spirit of Prophecy regarding the value and role of Bible study. The reader is encouraged to further study this important topic.

The word of God, spoken to the heart, has an animating power, and those who will frame any excuse for neglecting to become acquainted with it will neglect the claims of God in many respects. One of the prophets of God exclaims, "While I was musing, the fire burned." If Christians would earnestly search the Scriptures, more hearts would burn with the vivid truths therein revealed. Their hopes would brighten with the precious promises strewn like pearls all through the sacred writings. In contemplating the history of the patriarchs, the prophets, the men who loved and feared God and walked with him, hearts will glow with the spirit which animated these worthies. As the mind dwells upon the virtue and piety of holy men of old, the spirit which inspired them will kindle a flame of love and holy fervor in the hearts of those who would be like them in character. (*The Review and Herald*, November 28, 1878)

"'Search the Scriptures,' was the injunction of the Master. Many have lost much because they have neglected this duty. When we search the word of God, angels are by our side, reflecting bright beams of light upon its sacred pages. The Scriptures appeal to man as having power to choose between right and wrong; they speak to him in warning, in reproof, in entreaty, in encouragement. The mind must be exercised on the solemn truths of God's word, or it will grow weak. **We have the truth brought out in publications, but it is not enough to rely upon other men's thoughts. We must examine for ourselves, and learn the reasons of our faith by comparing scripture with scripture**. Take the Bible, and on your knees plead with God to enlighten your mind. If we would study the Bible diligently and prayerfully every day, we should every day see some beautiful truth in a new, clear, and forcible light." (*The Review and Herald*, March 4, 1884, emphassis supplied)

"Both old and young neglect the Bible. They do not make it their study, the rule of their life. Especially are the young guilty of this neglect. Most of them find time to read other books, but the book that points out the way to eternal life is not daily studied. Idle stories are attentively read, while the Bible is neglected. This book is our guide to a higher, holier life. The youth would pronounce it the most interesting book they ever read had not their imagination been perverted by the reading of fictitious stories." (*Counsels to Parents, Teachers, and Students*, 139)

"There is yet much precious truth to be revealed to the people in this time of peril and darkness, but **it is Satan's determined purpose to prevent the light of truth from shining into the hearts of men. If we would have the light that has been provided for us, we should show our desire for it by diligently searching the word of God**. Precious truths that have long been in obscurity are to be revealed in a light that will make manifest their sacred worth; for God will glorify His word, that it may appear in a light in which we have never before beheld it. But those who profess to love the truth must put to the stretch their powers, that they may comprehend the deep things of the word, that God may be glorified and His people may be blessed and enlightened. **With humble hearts, subdued by the grace of God, you should come to the task of searching the Scriptures, prepared to accept every ray of divine light, and to walk in the way of holiness.**" (*Counsels on Sabbath School Work*, 25, emphasis supplied)

"If I had an opportunity, I would speak to the students of every Sabbath school in the land, lifting up my voice in earnest appeal that they go to the word of God, seeking for truth and light. God has precious light to come to His people at this very time, and you should strive earnestly in your investigations to aim at nothing less than a thorough knowledge of every point of truth, that you may not be found in the day of God among those who have not lived by every word that proceedeth out of the mouth of God." (*Counsels on Sabbath School Work*, 31)

"God would have those who profess to be His followers thoroughly furnished with proof of the doctrines of His word. When and where can this be better obtained than in youth at the Sabbath school? Parents should in no case treat this matter indifferently." (*The Review and Herald*, November 28, 1878)

Chapter 5

"Interesting" vs. "Entertaining"

We have thus far seen the value and scriptural basis of the Family-integrated, Bible-study model for Sabbath school. Let us now turn our attention to some practical aspects of this model.

We are told, "Our Sabbath schools should be made more **interesting**." (*Counsels on Sabbath School Work*, 114)

To properly understand how our Sabbath schools should be made more interesting, as the above statement tells us to do, it is important to understand the difference between "interesting" and "entertaining." Because of our societal mindset and culture, we tend to think that to interest a child we need to entertain them. In fact, we tend to confuse the terms and make them synonymous. To the modern mindset, interesting and entertaining are almost the same. But there is a vast difference.

Entertaining refers to a performance, and is something that amuses or attracts the attention, but does not necessarily engage the mind. The attitude created in the hearer is generally one of *receiving*.

Interesting means that something is attracting the attention and making the individual want to learn more about something or to be involved in something. When something is interesting, *the mind is engaged* and the individual wants to learn more. The attitude of the participant here is one of *active engagement*.

Entertainment seeks to grab the attention and uses *external* means to captivate the listener, while something interesting will seek to make the student *internally* moti-vated to know more about the topic.

It is important that we *interest* our children, especial-ly in the study of the Bible, and we must be careful not to merely entertain them. We do not want an environ-ment or class that keeps their attention and feeds them information but does not engage their interest and mind. This will not affect a lasting change upon the heart and character.

God desires us to think and to engage the powers of mind that He has given us, while Satan desires to en-tertain us. Let us not think that we need to entertain our children to make them be interested, for these are two distinct methods.

In planning an interesting Sabbath school program, we do not need many activities and an exciting presenta-tion to grab the attention. This is based in entertainment, where the child or the student is to *receive* the program and the instruction, rather than in *interest* where the mind is engaged.

So, how do we get our children to be *interested*? Do we have a definition or further description of what the Spirit of Prophecy means by "interesting"? Thankfully, we do. Let us turn our attention to a paragraph which explains what is meant by *interesting*.

"It should be the special object of the heads of the family to make the hour of worship intensely interest-ing. By a little thought and careful preparation for this season, when we come into the presence of God, family worship can be made pleasant and will be fraught with results that eternity alone will reveal. Let the father se-lect a portion of Scripture that is interesting and easily understood; a few verses will be sufficient to furnish a lesson which may be studied and practiced through the day. Questions may be asked, a few earnest, interesting remarks made, or incident, short and to the point, may be brought in by way of illustration. At least a few verses of spirited song may be sung, and the prayer offered should be short and pointed." (*Child Guidance*, 521)

Let us examine this paragraph in detail.

"It should be the special object of the heads of the family to make the hour of worship **intensely interesting**...."

This paragraph is specifically speaking of family worship, but the principles apply to the Sabbath school too, especially considering that a good family Sabbath school will be an extension of what is happening in family worship. Notice, it says *intensely interesting*. So, the description to follow will be an excellent example of a program designed to generate interest. Let us continue.

"...By a little **thought and careful preparation** for this season, when we come into the presence of God, family worship can be made pleasant and will be fraught with results that eternity alone will reveal...."

What is needed to make a class interesting? Thought and preparation. This is vitally important for the teacher to do. Similar instruction is given in the book *Education*. "To make such a service what it should be [speaking of the time of worship], thought should be given to preparation." (*Education*, 186) And in *Counsels on Sabbath School Work* we are told: "Let them lay plans to make a practical application of the lesson, and awaken an interest in the minds and hearts of the children under their charge. Let the activities of the scholars find scope in solving the problems of Bible truth. The teachers may give character to the work, so that the exercises will not be dry and uninteresting." (*Counsels on Sabbath School Work*, 113)

"...Let the father **select a portion of Scripture that is interesting and easily understood; a few verses** will be sufficient to furnish a lesson which may be studied and practiced through the day...."

Where should the reading be taken from? From the Scriptures. Should it be a long portion of Scripture? No, to keep it interesting, just a portion of Scripture should be selected, a few verses being sufficient for thorough study, discussion, and practical application. We need not cram extensive amounts of material into our Sabbath school programs. It is better to dig deeply into a topic over a period of several weeks rather than to try to cover too much in one class.

"...**Questions** may be asked..."

Jesus used this method often. Asking questions will encourage participation and get the class thinking and will generate interest more than almost any other method.

"...A few earnest, interesting remarks made, or incident, short and to the point, may be brought in by way of **illustration**...."

Jesus used illustration frequently, especially through parables and stories. We are told of Christ's teaching, "The unknown was illustrated by the known; sacred and divine truths, by natural, earthly things, with which the people were most familiar. These were the things that would speak to their hearts, and make the deepest impression on their minds." (*Counsels to Parents, Teachers, and Students*, 178) A good teacher will give examples or bring out object lessons from everyday life. We read in the book Education, "The teacher . . . should teach largely by illustration, and even in dealing with older pupils should be careful to make every explanation plain and clear." (*Education*, 233)

"…At least a few verses of **spirited song** may be sung…"

Singing is an important part of worship and Sabbath school and is part of an interesting program.

"…And **the prayer offered should be short and pointed**."

Sabbath school is not the place for long, drawn-out prayer sessions. Let the prayers be short and to the point.

In the above paragraph that we have analyzed we see an explanation of what is meant by "interesting." It is important that when we apply the counsel to make Sabbath school intensely interesting we use God's definition of interesting rather than our modern, entertainment-based cultural definition.

Also, as mentioned earlier, the stories of the Bible are an excellent method of capturing interest. In the book *Education*, page 185, we read, "In all that men have written, where can be found anything that has such a hold upon the heart, anything so well adapted to awaken the interest of the little ones, as the stories of the Bible?" (*Education*, 185)

To review, here are six keys for an interesting Sabbath school program.

1. Give sufficient thought and preparation.
2. Use a portion of Scripture (which should include Bible stories).
3. Ask questions.
4. Use illustrations.
5. Sing songs.
6. Have short and pointed prayer.

Chapter 6

Tips for Teachers

What are some practical methods for teaching an age-integrated Bible-study class and engaging everyone? Let us consider some important tips for teachers.

1. Discard the traditional idea of a "teacher".

For the family-integrated Sabbath school model, the traditional method of the teacher standing up in front of the class delivering information to the students sitting in neat little rows is not the most effective. The members of the class will be far more engaged when the teacher acts more as a "facilitator" or "class leader" in a round-table format. Keeping the students engaged is vital, and even the most interesting presentation by a speaker from the front of the class cannot achieve full student engagement and involvement, because even if the student is interested he is merely listening. A presentation may be improved by the teacher asking questions, but even this has been shown by scientific research to achieve only limited engagement compared to a round-table format where the "teacher" acts more as a discussion leader.

The model of teaching that Jesus followed is instructive to us. Notice the description of Jesus' method of teaching given us in the book *Education*.

Sometimes He taught them as they sat together on the mountainside, sometimes beside the sea, or from the fisherman's boat, sometimes as they walked by the way. Whenever He spoke to the multitude, the disciples formed the inner circle. They pressed close beside Him, that they might lose nothing of His instruction. They were attentive listeners, eager to understand the truths they were to teach in all lands and to all ages." (*Education, 85)*

While the Sabbath school teacher may not be able to spend all week with the class as Jesus did, the principle is the same in that class time with Jesus was not a scheduled event where the disciples sat in rows and Jesus gave them a lecture from the front. They gathered around Jesus.

2. Gather the thoughts of others.

Teaching Sabbath school is not a venue for the teacher to give a presentation of his/her personal ideas and studies on a topic. While the teacher's thoughts are valuable, Sabbath school should not be merely a presentation; it should be a group study. Rather than only giving his/her thoughts, the facilitator should encourage others, both young and old, to share their thoughts. As a teacher, you may need to hold yourself back at times! Be sure that all have the opportunity to share in the class. Aim for full engagement of all the students.

"It is not the best plan for teachers to do all the talking, but they should draw out the class to tell what they know. Then let the teacher, with a few brief, pointed remarks or illustrations, impress the lesson upon their minds. (*Testimonies on Sabbath-School Work,* 18, 19)

While teachers can certainly share a particular gem of truth or point that they have gleaned as part of their study and preparation to teach, a better method to engage the students is to lead the class in a study to help them make the same discovery. As teachers prepare for the class, they should consider the process of thought and study by which they gained that special gem of truth and develop a way to lead their students through the same process. This is another reason why it is important to take time for thought and preparation ahead of time.

3. Engage everyone.

A good teacher makes sure no one is left out and seeks to engage every individual. There are many ways to engage everyone. Here are a few ideas.

Ask questions directly. While there is nothing wrong with asking a question to the class in general, many class members are too shy or timid to give an answer without being asked directly. A good teacher watches for those who may have something to share but are too timid to speak without being asked directly. While we should be careful not to make someone feel uncomfortable or "on-the-spot", asking someone a direct question may help him/her feel appreciated and know that their contribution is valued. It can also help an otherwise unengaged individual to learn how to participate.

Watch for those who are drifting. Occasionally, a young person (or older one!) may start daydreaming or otherwise become unengaged. A good teacher will watch for this and help engage the child by asking him a question, asking him to read the next Bible verse in the lesson, or asking for his thoughts on the subject being discussed.

Read the Bible verses. Even the familiar Bible verses associated with the lesson should be read. There is power in God's word, and we want to tap into that power. Reading the Bible verses also connects what is learned in Sabbath school class with the Scriptures, embedding God's Word into the mind. It also helps familiarize all with God's Word. And, taking the time to read the verses gives the message that those verses are important. If the Bible passage is long, split it up allowing several people to help with the reading.

Encourage participation. Encourage participation. Participating in something engages the mind and piques the interest in a way that simply listening to something cannot. Going around the room giving each one in the class a turn to read the Bible passages, sections in the lesson, or sections in the Spirit of Prophecy helps encourage participation and tends to keep all minds engaged more than asking for volunteers or assigning readers. Connecting part of the lesson or a Bible verse with a song, and singing the song, can help all to participate.

Give special help for non-reader and those who are timid. To engage those who cannot read, include a few simple questions that the littlest ones can answer. You may be surprised at how much a little one is absorbing in the class. And be sure you take notice of which children are more timid than others. Encourage their participation by occasionally asking them questions and asking for their thoughts.

4. Show interest and enthusiasm.

Enthusiasm is contagious. Young children naturally become enthusiastic about what they see the adults in their lives excited about. When the entire class is enthusiastic, a child cannot help but enjoy the class.

"An important element in educational work is enthusiasm. On this point there is a useful suggestion in a remark once made by a celebrated actor. The archbishop of Canterbury had put to him the question why actors in a play affect their audiences so powerfully by speaking of things imaginary, while ministers of the gospel often affect theirs so little by speaking of things real. 'With due submission to your grace,' replied the actor, 'permit me to say that the reason is plain: It lies in the power of enthusiasm. We on the stage speak of things imaginary as if they were real, and you in the pulpit speak of things real as if they were imaginary.'" (*Education*, 233)

Are we demonstrating an interest in the things we want our children and youth to be interested in? If we approach the Sabbath school lesson with a lackluster attitude, can we expect more from our youth?

"Let the teachers show that they have thoroughly learned the lesson, and are intensely interested in it." (*Testimonies on Sabbath-School Work*, 110)

5. Don't just read the lesson.

While it's fine to read sections of the lesson that will be particularly helpful for the class, people tend to "zone-out" when someone starts reading. To keep minds engaged, try to avoid simply reading through the entire lesson during Sabbath school time.

"In some [Sabbath] schools, I am sorry to say, the custom prevails of reading the lesson from the lesson sheet. This should not be. It need not be, if the time that is often needlessly and even sinfully employed, were given to the study of the Scriptures. There is no reason why Sabbath-school lessons should be less perfectly learned by teachers or pupils than are the lessons of the day school. They should be better learned, as they treat of subjects infinitely more important. A neglect here is displeasing to God." (*Testimonies on Sabbath-School Work*, 10)

"Every teacher, before he stands at the head of his class, should have his plans distinctly laid out in his mind as to what he wants to do for that day and on that occasion. Reciting a lesson yourself before the class is not teaching it; you want simple words and plainly, clearly stated ideas. Make sure that your scholars understand you. If they cannot comprehend your ideas, then your labor is lost. Do not skim the surface; work deep." (*Testimonies on Sabbath-School Work*, 24)

"Jesus has said, 'Search the Scriptures; for in them ye think ye have eternal life: and they are they which testify of Me.' Do not encourage a superficial manner of investigating the truth. Make every point of truth clear and distinct to the minds of the children. Do not crowd upon their minds an accumulated amount of matter at one time." (*Counsels on Sabbath School Work*, 112)

Families should be encouraged to read the lesson at home (during family worship, during homeschool time, or any other time that works for the individual families); then, when the children come to Sabbath school, they will be familiar with the material covered in the lesson and will be able to be more engaged in the study.

Here are a few ideas for approaches other than reading the lesson in class:

Tell the story in your own words. Just cover the highlights. Make it short and sweet so you don't lose interest.

Have the class tell the story. Begin the story with an introduction, and then ask someone in the class, "What happened next?" Then ask someone else, "Then what happened?" Then ask another person, "And then what happened?" You can also throw in a few thought questions as you go, such as "How do you think that made [the person in the story] feel?" "What would you think if you were in that situation?"

Combine telling the story with reading short passages from the Spirit of Prophecy and the Bible. This helps the adults have deeper understanding, while still engaging children.

Skip telling the story and ask questions about it instead. If almost everyone has already read the story throughout the week, you can skip telling it and instead ask questions about the story. Questions are a great way to instantly engage everyone's brains. With sufficient, well-worded questions, even those who didn't read the story will know it fairly well by the time you reach the end of the questions. If you need help coming up with questions, think "who, what, why, when, where."

6. Make the lessons simple, practical, and relevant.

Another tip for Sabbath school teachers is to make the lessons simple, practical, and relevant. There are many fundamental teachings and doctrines of the Scriptures that can be learned through the stories of the Bible. If the teacher is willing to give time and thought to preparation, studying the lesson from the Bible and the Spirit of Prophecy ahead of time, God will help him/her to present the lessons of the Bible stories in their simplicity so that both young and old will benefit from the same class.

"What a blessing it would be if all would teach as Jesus taught! He did not aim to attract attention by eloquence or by overwhelming grandeur of sentiment. On the contrary, His language was plain, and His thoughts were expressed with greatest simplicity; but He spoke with loving earnestness. **In your teaching be as near like Him as possible**." (*Testimonies on Sabbath- School Work*, 110, emphasis supplied)

The teacher should seek to impart more than mere knowledge. Knowledge without practical application will do the class participants little good. A good teacher will help all to make practical application of the points and lessons learned.

"It is not enough even to have knowledge. We must have ability to use the knowledge aright." (*The Ministry of Healing*, 449)

The teacher should also think of ways to make the lesson relevant and understandable. For example, when studying the story of Nebuchadnezzar's image, help the children grasp how tall the image was by comparing it to a nearby tall tree or something else that they have seen and are familiar with. When studying the story of Jesus feeding 5,000 people, help the children comprehend how many people that is by figuring how long a line of 5,000 people would be (about 1 1/2 miles). When studying about the writing on the wall in the book of Daniel, bring a brick to class and ask for volunteers to try to write on the brick with their fingers.

If you don't think you are creative enough to come up with ideas, ask the Lord for help. He is faithful to help every time!

7. Keep the correct goal in mind.

Remember that your goal is to encourage all in the class to seek for a deeper knowledge of Scripture and a closer relationship with God. The goal is not to "get through the lesson". Don't try to cover too much. It is more important that the subject matter is understood and applied than it is to merely cover the information in the lesson.

"Do not encourage a superficial manner of investigating the truth. Make every point of truth clear and distinct to the minds of the children." (*Counsels on Sabbath School Work*, 112)

"We must search the Scriptures, not merely rush through a chapter and repeat it, taking no pains to understand it, but we must dig for the jewel of truth which will enrich the mind, and fortify the soul against the wiles and temptations of the archdeceiver." (*Counsels on Sabbath School Work*, 19)

"A mere superficial reading of the inspired word will be of little advantage." (*Christian Education*, 100)

Remember also to keep the focus on things of eternal importance. Make clear and simple the points which you want to bring out. There are many interesting topics that could be studied, but are they of eternal significance? Do they encourage all in the class in a deeper knowledge of Scripture and a closer relationship with God?

"[Jesus] might have unlocked mysteries that have required centuries of toil and study to penetrate. He might have made suggestions in scientific lines that, till the close of time, would have afforded food for thought and stimulus for invention. But He did not do this. He said nothing to gratify curiosity or to stimulate selfish ambition. He did not deal in abstract theories, but in that which is essential to the development of character; that which will enlarge man's capacity for knowing God, and increase his power to do good. He spoke of those truths that relate to the conduct of life and that unite man with eternity." (*Education*, 81)

"Christ…would not spare a moment from teaching the science of salvation. His time, His faculties, and His life were appreciated and used only as the means for working out the salvation of the souls of men. He had come to seek and to save that which was lost, and He would not be turned from His purpose. He allowed nothing to divert Him. (*The Ministry of Healing*, 448)

The purpose of Sabbath school is also not to provide a venue for deep theological discussion. These can be conducted with a separate study group at a different time. The Sabbath school should be a means of interesting and involving all the class participants in the study of the word of God.

8. Listen to comments with interest.

Everyone's thoughts and comments are valuable. Listen to the comments of the playful three-year-old with as much interest as you do the comments of the wise elder of the church. Children notice when others are interested in what they have to say, and this will encourage them to actively participate.

When comments are made which do not relate to the point at hand or are distracting from the important spiritual lessons being studied, you may kindly and tactfully redirect the conversation while still respecting and appreciating everyone.

9. Use caution in correcting.

Clearly, we don't want to allow error to be taught in a Sabbath school class; yet much caution, gentleness, and tact should be used when correcting someone, and much consideration should be given as to whether a correction is needed at all.. Children especially need to feel free to speak without the fear that they will be criticized for a wrong answer – or they may soon stop trying to answer. Encourage study and point to scriptures which reveal the truth of the matter rather than criticizing or meeting error with your own thoughts and opinions.

The adults of the class can encourage truth and discourage error by their own example. They should avoid sharing their opinions, their ideas, or "what I have always believed" when commenting. Instead, share the truth as it is found in the Scriptures. Present the pure truth as it is found in a "thus sayeth the Lord."

10. Give an assignment for the following week.

At the end of class, consider giving an assignment for the following week. This keeps the children engaged, keeps interest levels high, and can also help them apply what is learned in a practical way.

For example, when studying about Creation, ask participants to come to next week's class with their favorite evidence for Creation vs evolution. When studying about Jonah, assign the class participants to find Joppa, Nineveh, and Tarshish on a map and measure the distance between them.

For Sabbath school classes that are an hour in length, the first ten to twenty minutes could be spent in going over the assignment for the previous week. This sets a very engaging tone for the rest of the class.

Chapter 7

Qualifications of Teachers

The role of Sabbath school teacher is a solemn and important one. We are told, "It requires holy men, men who have humility, who are abiding in Christ, to be educators of our youth in the Sabbath school." (*Counsels on Sabbath School Work*, 64) Much instruction is given as to the qualifications and responsibilities of Sabbath school teachers. Some points are mentioned here, and the reader is invited to continue further study on the topic.

"For Christ's sake let the teachers and the leading workers in your Sabbath school be men and women who love and fear God; men and women who realize the responsibility of their position, as those who are watching for souls and must render an account to God for the influence they exert over those under their charge." (*Counsels on Sabbath School Work*, 71)

1. The teacher must be a student of the Word of God.

Sabbath school teachers must be earnest, deep students of the word of God. It is not sufficient to merely read the comments and thoughts of others in regard to the Bible. Teachers must deeply drink from the fountain of truth directly in order to correctly instruct others.

"Teachers in the Sabbath-school have a missionary field given them to teach the Scriptures, not, parrot like, to repeat over that which they have taken no pains to understand if teachers are not imbued with the spirit of truth, and care not for the knowledge of what is revealed in the word of God, how can they present the truth in an attractive light to those under their charge? The prayer of Christ for his disciples was, Sanctify them through thy truth; thy word is truth. If we are to be sanctified through a knowledge of the truth found in the word of God, we must have an intelligent knowledge of his will therein revealed. We must search the Scriptures, not merely rush through a chapter and repeat it, taking no pains to understand it, but we must dig for the jewel of truth which will enrich the mind, and fortify the soul against the wiles and temptations of the arch-deceiver." (*The Review and Herald*, November 28, 1878)

"If you are called to be a teacher in any branch of the work of God, you are called also to be a learner in the school of Christ. If you take upon you the sacred responsibility of teaching others, you take upon you the duty of going to the bottom of every subject you seek to teach. If you present a subject from the word of God to your pupils in the Sabbath school, you should make the reasons for your faith so plain that your scholars shall be convinced of its truth. You should diligently search and compare the evidences of the word of God on messages that He sends to the church, that you may know what is truth, and be able to direct those who look to you into the way of righteousness." (*Counsels on Sabbath School Work*, 31)

"Let the teachers themselves drink deep of the water of salvation, and the angels of God will minister to them, and they will know just what course the Lord would have them take to win the precious youth to Jesus. It requires aptitude, a will, perseverance, a spirit such as Jacob had when he wrestled in prayer, and exclaimed, "I will not let Thee go, except Thou bless me." When the blessing of God rests upon the teachers, it can but be reflected to those under their charge. Never place the youth under individuals who are spiritually indolent, who have no high, elevated, holy aspirations; for the same mind of indifference, pharisaism, of form without the power, will be seen in both teachers and scholars." (*Testimonies on Sabbath-School Work*, 13)

2. The true teacher seeks to impart more than mere intellectual knowledge.

The true teacher of the Sabbath school will seek to impart more than mere intellectual knowledge. He desires the Word of God to take root in the hearts of the students, springing up and bearing fruit in lasting change. He labors for the transformation of character and true conversion in his students, rather than head-knowledge alone. He works in simplicity and with a true love for souls.

"A mere intellectual understanding of the word of God will not be sufficient to influence the habits of the life, for the life is regulated by the condition of the heart. When Sabbath school teachers have taught the lessons of external revelation, their work is but just begun, and they should not cease their labor until they have evidence that the precepts of heaven are not only accepted by the understanding of the pupil, but written upon the heart." (*Testimonies on Sabbath-School Work*, 57, 58)

"There should be much personal work done in the Sabbath school. The necessity of this kind of work is not recognized and appreciated as it should be. From a heart filled with gratitude for the love of God, which has been imparted to the soul, the teacher should labor tenderly and earnestly for the conversion of his scholars." (*Counsels on Sabbath School Work*, 61)

"A true educator will carry the minds of his hearers with him. His words will be few but earnest. Coming from the heart, they will be full of sympathy, and warm with the love for precious souls. His educational advantages may have been limited, and he may have but little natural ability, but a love for the work and a willingness to labor in humility will enable him to awaken a deep interest in both teachers and scholars. The hearts of the young will be drawn to him. His work will not be a mere form. He may have the ability to draw out from both teachers and students precious gems of spiritual and intellectual truths, and thus, while educating others, he will be educated himself. The scholars are not awed by his display of profound knowledge, and in simple language they tell what impression the lesson has made upon their minds. The result is a deep and living interest in the school. Through the simplicity of the gospel of Christ, he has reached them where they are. Their hearts are melted, and now he can mold them into the image of his Master." (*Counsels on Sabbath School Work*, 167)

3. **The teacher must be transformed by the truths he teaches and exemplify Christ in their life.**

The Sabbath school teacher must exemplify in his own life what he seeks for in his students. If he desires the Word to take root in his student's hearts, must not the same Word take root in his own heart and bear fruit? If he is seeking character transformation in the lives of his students, should not he himself experience the genuine converting power of the gospel? There is much counsel written on this topic, and the reader is asked to consider the following statements carefully and deeply.

"The teacher can gain the respect of his pupils in no other way than by revealing in his own character the principles which he seeks to teach them." (*Counsels on Sabbath School Work*, 102)

"Without Me,' Christ says, 'ye can do nothing.' Then of what value would be the teaching of one who knew nothing by personal experience of the power of Christ? It would be a great inconsistency to urge such a one to take a class in the Sabbath school, but it is even worse to permit a class to be under the influence of a teacher whose dress and deportment deny the Saviour, whom he professes to serve.

Those who teach in Sabbath school must have their hearts warmed and invigorated by the truth of God, being not hearers only, but also doers of the Word. They should be nourished in Christ as the branches are nourished in the vine. The dews of heavenly grace should fall upon them, that their hearts may be like precious plants, whose buds open and expand and give forth a grateful fragrance, as flowers in the garden of God. Teachers should be diligent students of the word of God, and ever reveal the fact that they are learning daily lessons in the school of Christ, and are able to communicate to others the light they have received from Him who is the Great Teacher, the Light of the world. Teachers should feel their responsibility, and make use of every opportunity to improve, that they may render the best kind of service in a manner that will result in the salvation of souls.

Both teachers and pupils should awake to the importance of manifesting industry and perseverance in the study of God's word. They should be much in communion with God, where petty temptations will not control them, and indolence and apathy will be successfully resisted. No idleness, no self-indulgence should be allowed by those who profess to be Christian workers." (*Testimonies on Sabbath-School Work*, 54, 55)

"Every Sabbath school worker who has passed from death unto life through the transforming grace of Christ, will reveal the deep moving of the Spirit of God upon his own heart. Those who attempt to direct others, who make a pretension of guiding souls to the path of holiness, while their own life is marked with pleasure loving, with pride, and with love of display, are unfaithful servants. Their life is not in accordance with their profession; their influence is an offense to God. They need a thorough conversion. Their hearts are so filled up with rubbish that there is no room for ennobling, elevated truth. The soul temple needs to be refined, purified, cleansed; for Satan rather than God is abiding in the heart.

It is essential that care should be taken when placing men and women in positions of trust. You should know something in regard to their past life, and the character that has been developed. **You would better double your classes under God-fearing workers than to multiply teachers whose influence is not in accordance with the holy character of truth which we profess, for their influence will be demoralizing**." (Testimonies on Sabbath-School Work, 22-26)

"You who are engaged in the work as Sabbath school superintendents and teachers remember that though you may teach the Word fluently, this is not all that is necessary. You may have plans whereby you hope to make your mark; but before you carry them out, ask yourself, Will it prove to be the mark of Christ, or a revelation of myself?

Much cheap machinery is used in Sabbath schools. How many people have been accepted as Sabbath school instructors who have never surrendered the soul to the discipline of Christ? They refuse to accept Christ, yet they accept the position of a teacher of Bible truth. There are those who step into the ranks as volunteer workers who have known the reasons of our faith from their youth up, but whose characters have never been transformed. They bear no sweet, precious fruit. They may be looked upon as excellent teachers, but their teaching has about as much influence as a recitation of the multiplication table would have. They are signboards pointing in the wrong direction. They have never realized what the true aim of life is. They have missed the mark most decidedly, and are no more fit to teach than were the foolish virgins to go into the marriage supper of the Lamb.

Let every Sabbath school teacher remember that he must bear about with him the precious fragrance of Christ's grace. The Sabbath school is a missionary field, open for all who love God. Into this work men and women may put heart-piety and soul-burdened, loving service. Those who do this, work to a purpose. The greatest earnestness, the deepest spirituality, are demanded for a Sabbath school worker. The simplicity of true religion, cherished in the hearts of superintendents and teachers, will bring angels of heaven into the school to impress and win souls.

Sabbath school superintendents and teachers should drink every day of the water of life. Then they will have within them a well of water, constantly springing up unto everlasting life. They are themselves learners in the school of the great Teacher, and therefore they can bring from the treasure house of the Word things new and old. The love of Christ speaks from the lips and is expressed in the countenance.

Such teachers show their love for Christ by their love for His children. They carry their students upon their soul until they are gathered into the fold, adopted as sons and daughters of God. They do not rest until they see before them the practical results of their work. They yearn for the souls committed to their charge. They will not rest until the Lord answers their earnest prayer for the conversion of souls. Angels of God co-operate with such teachers, enabling them to do service for the Master. The light of the Sun of Righteousness shines naturally from the soul. The words they speak are received as sincerity and truth. Christians indeed, they are doing the work of Christ, under His supervision." (Letters and Manuscripts 14, Manuscript 45, 1899)

"The truly converted laborer in the Sabbath-school will not be moulded after the customs and practices of the world, but will stand in moral independence. He will set an example that will be consistent with his profession, coming out from the world, and maintaining a separation from its spirit and fashions. He will not be turned in the least from his steadfast purpose to be one with Christ, nor yield an iota from his stand of fidelity to God, in opposition to pride, to indulgence in selfish amusement, to expenditure of means for the gratification of inclination or love of display, but will be an example in spirit, deportment, and dress.

Sabbath-school worker, which will you meet, the standard of Christ or that of the world? Oh, will you say,

"I will lift the cross and follow Jesus?" Will you not cultivate His tenderness in persuasion, His earnestness in exhortation, and exemplify the exalted principles of the truth, manifesting in life and character what the religion of Christ has done for you? Shall we not all heed the exhortation of the apostle, 'Put ye on the Lord Jesus Christ, and make not provision for the flesh, to fulfil the lusts thereof'?

There is need of representing genuine religion before the youth. Such religion will prove a vital power, an all-pervading influence. From heartfelt devotion, joyousness, freshness, and continual growth, will spring, and this is the religion that the youth must behold if they are to be drawn to Christ. This kind of religion will leave its divine impression upon souls, and its possessor will be renewed both mentally and physically by the refreshing grace of God.

Try it for one year, you who are educators and teachers in our Sabbath and day schools, and see if you will not be able to say, "The Lord hath wrought wondrously for us, for many souls have been brought to the Master, as precious sheaves for the heavenly garner." (*Sabbath-School Worker,* December 1, 1891)

"It is our own character and experience that determine our influence upon others. In order to convince others of the power of Christ's grace, we must know its power in our own hearts and lives. The gospel we present for the saving of souls must be the gospel by which our own souls are saved. Only through a living faith in Christ as a personal Saviour is it possible to make our influence felt in a skeptical world. If we would draw sinners out of the swift-running current, our own feet must be firmly set upon the Rock, Christ Jesus. The badge of Christianity is not an outward sign, not the wearing of a cross or a crown, but it is that which reveals the union of man with God. By the power of His grace manifested in the transformation of character the world is to be convinced that God has sent His Son as its Redeemer. No other influence that can surround the human soul has such power as the influence of an unselfish life. The strongest argument in favor of the gospel is a loving and lovable Christian." *(Testimonies on Sabbath-School Work*, 115, 116)

4. The teacher must be connected with the Lord.

To accomplish his work, to impart heavenly wisdom to his students, and to experience in himself and encourage in others character transformation, the teacher *must* be connected with the Source of wisdom and power. If the teacher is not much in prayer and communion with the Lord and constantly connected with Him, the teacher's work will be in vain.

"Teachers and workers in every department of the Sabbath school work, I address you in the fear of God, and tell you that unless you have a living connection with God, and are often before Him in earnest prayer, you will not be able to do your work with heavenly wisdom, and win souls for Christ. (*Counsels on Sabbath School Work*, 75)

"A keen, sharp intellect may be an advantage, but the power of the educator is in his heart connection with the Light and Life of the world....He will not be great in his own estimation, neither will he seek constantly to bolster up and strengthen his own dignity; but the humility of Jesus will be personified in his life. He will feel the truth of the words of Christ, 'Without Me ye can do nothing.' Such teachers as these are greatly needed. **God will work with them**. 'Learn of Me,' says Christ, 'for I am meek and lowly in heart.'" (*Counsels on Sabbath School Work*, 168, emphasis supplied)

5. The teacher must care deeply for the students and seek a relationship with them.

"The teacher's obligations are weighty and sacred, but no part of the work is more important than to look after the youth with tender, loving solicitude, that they may feel that we have a friend in them. Once gain their confidence, and you can lead them, control them, and train them easily. The holy motives of our Christian principles must be brought into our life. The salvation of our pupils is the highest interest entrusted to the God-fearing teacher. He is Christ's worker, and his special and determined effort should be to save souls from perdition and win them to Jesus Christ. God will require this at the hands of teachers. Every one should lead a life of piety, of purity, of painstaking effort in the discharge of every duty. If the heart is glowing with the love of God, there will be pure affection, which is essential; prayers will be fervent, and faithful warnings will be given. Neglect these, and the souls under your charge are endangered. Better spend less time in long speeches, or in absorbing study, and attend to these neglected duties." (*Counsels on Sabbath School Work*, 122)

Question: Shall we include the youth as teachers?

Considering the great importance of having spiritually-strong Sabbath school teachers, the question is naturally raised, shall the youth be included in the responsibilities of Sabbath school? Can they be given an opportunity to teach? How can they develop experience? Most certainly, the youth can and should be included in the leadership of Sabbath school.

"In our Sabbath schools the Christian youth should be entrusted with responsibilities, that they may develop their abilities and gain spiritual power. Let the youth first give themselves to God, and then let them in their early experience be taught to help others. We must educate the youth, that they may learn how to work for the salvation of souls; and in educating the youth for this work, we shall also learn how to labor more successfully, becoming efficient agents in the hands of God for the conversion of our scholars." (*Counsels on Sabbath School Work*, 62)

Notice, the youth, "should be entrusted with responsibilities, that they may develop their abilities and gain spiritual power." We are told that "skill is gained in the work itself" (*Education*, 268). Our youth certainly should be given opportunity to lead in Sabbath school, but notice what the prerequisite was in the above statement: "Let the youth first give themselves to God." (*Counsels on Sabbath School Work*, 62) This is essential, as we read in the following paragraphs.

"Christian teachers and students are responsible to God for the gracious privileges they enjoy, for they are to be laborers together with God, bearing a decided testimony to the power of God's saving grace in the sight of earth and heaven. The efficiency and influence of the workers for God will be in proportion to their moral elevation and purity. One Christian student who receives the Word of

God may be the means of blessing his fellow-students. He can be a benefit to others if, patiently and kindly and interestingly, he will go over the lesson with those who do not take an interest in the things of God, and will make his instruction simple and definite. This kind of work will require the exercise of wisdom from above, that the worker may approach in an acceptable manner those who most need help, and lead them to Christ, where the wants of the soul may be satisfied....

When the youth is converted, do not leave him in idleness; give him something to do in the vineyard of the Master. According to his ability, let him be employed; for the Lord has given to every man his work. (*Testimonies on Sabbath-School Work*, 51)

The principle we find is that the knowledge and information an individual possesses, youth or adult, is not, in the eyes of God, the most important qualification for teaching. What the Lord needs are those who are committed to Him. Young or old, if the individual realizes their dependence upon God and are committed to him, they can safely be trusted with the role of teacher.

"Do not refuse to bear responsibilities because you have a sense of your weakness and inefficiency. God can give you strength and wisdom if you are consecrated to Him and keep humble." (*Counsels on Sabbath School Work*, 70)

"**If any one thinks he is capable** of teaching in the Sabbath school or in the day school the science of education, **he needs first to learn the fear of the Lord**, which is the beginning of wisdom, that he may teach this the highest of all sciences. (*Fundamentals of Christian Education*, 272, emphasis supplied)

If we think we are capable, we are most unqualified.

"A teacher's advantages may have been limited, so that he may not possess as high literary qualifications as might be desirable; yet if he has true insight into human nature; if he has a genuine love for his work, an appreciation of its magnitude, and a determination to improve; if he is willing to labor earnestly and perseveringly, he will comprehend the needs of his pupils, and, by his sympathetic, progressive spirit, will inspire them to follow as he seeks to lead them onward and upward He who discerns the opportunities and privileges of his work will allow nothing to stand in the way of earnest endeavor for self-improvement. He will spare no pains to reach the highest standard of excellence. All that he desires his pupils to become, he will himself strive to be. (*Testimonies on Sabbath-School Work*, 118, 119)

Chapter 8

The Role of the Parents

While the role of the teacher of a Sabbath school class is vitally important, parents play an even greater role in helping their children and youth be interested in the study of the Bible and the science of salvation. The Family Bible-Study Sabbath School class provides parents with more opportunity to disciple and engage with their children in spiritual matters than in the traditional age-segregated Sabbath school environment. Yet this will require intentional effort on the part of the parents to accomplish.

"While it is essential that wise, patient efforts should be made by the teacher, the work must not be left altogether to the Sabbath-school and church worker, but it must find its foundation and support in the work of the home. Parents have a sacred responsibility and charge committed to them, and they are called upon to keep their charge, to bear their responsibility in the fear of God, watching for the souls of their children as they who must give an account." (*Sabbath School Worker*, April 1, 1889)

Here are several points on the role of the parents in the Sabbath school.

1. Show interest.
Just as the teacher must show an interest in the study in order to interest his pupils, so must the parent demonstrate practically that they are deeply interested in the

lesson. This interest is not an act, but a calm and genuine interest in these topics of eternal import that shows itself plainly in the daily life. Children arc great emulators, as well as accurate detectors of hypocrisy. *They will recognize and emulate the genuine interest by their parents in spiritual matters, just as they will lose interest in a religion which is of so little value as to hold their parents' interest for but one day per week.*

"The Sabbath school affords precious opportunities and privileges for the young. Parents should highly prize these advantages, and show their children that they appreciate them. **If they manifest no decided interest in the school themselves, they cannot expect their children to do so**. In the Sabbath school, parents may be learners as well as the children." (*Counsels on Sabbath School Work*, 52, emphasis supplied)

"Parents plead trifling excuses for not interesting themselves in the lessons with their children, and they fail to become conversant with the Scriptures. Fathers as well as mothers excuse themselves from disciplining their own minds. They do not seek first the kingdom of God and his righteousness, but exalt the temporal above the spiritual and eternal. This forgetfulness of God and neglect of his word is the example they give their children, which molds their minds after the worldly standard and not after the exalted standard erected by Christ." (*The Review and Herald*, November 28, 1878)

"As a preparation for teaching His precepts, God commands that they be hidden in the hearts of the parents.... **In order to interest our children in the Bible, we ourselves must be interested in it. To awaken in them a love for its study, we must love it. Our instruction to**

them will have only the weight of influence given it by our own example and spirit." (*Education*, 187, emphasis supplied)

So, who is to blame if the children and youth are not interested in spiritual things?

2. Study the Scriptures with their children.

"Fathers and mothers, we entreat you to take up your long-neglected duties. Search the Scriptures yourselves; assist your children in the study of the sacred word. Make diligent work because of past neglect. **Do not send the children away by themselves to study the Bible, but read it with them, teach them in a simple manner what you know, and keep in the school of Christ as diligent students yourselves**. Be determined that this work shall not be neglected. … Follow Christ's injunction, "Search the Scriptures," then you will advance in spiritual strength yourselves, and be able to instruct your children so that they need not come to the Sabbath-school untaught." (*The Review and Herald, November 28, 1878*, emphasis supplied)

"Parents should search the Scriptures with their children. They should become familiar with the lessons themselves; then they can assist their children in learning them. Every day some portion of time should be appropriated to the study of the lessons, not merely in learning to mechanically repeat the words, while the mind does not comprehend the meaning; but to go to the very foundation, and become familiar with what is brought out in the lesson. The indifference of the children, in very many cases, is chargeable to the parents. They are indifferent, and the children catch the same spirit. If parents show that they attach importance to the Sabbath school, by giving it respect and prominence, the children will generally copy their example." (*Counsels on Sabbath School Work*, 53)

"Let parents do their part, not only helping the children in their study, but becoming familiar with the lessons themselves. The Bible is our textbook. Parents, teachers, and scholars need to become better acquainted with the precious truths contained in both the Old and the New Testaments." (*Testimonies on Sabbath-School Work*, 14)

3. Connect the lesson with family worship.

Ideally, the Family Bible-Study Sabbath School class should be integrated into the family's worship throughout the week. The Spirit of Prophecy speaks much about parents doing the lessons with their children during the week. In God's plan the Sabbath school is not a drop off babysitter for the children on Sabbath mornings, nor an entertainment program for the young people, but rather it should be *an extension and continuation of what the family has been doing all week.*

If the entire family have been studying the lesson together throughout the week, the entire family can then take part in the class on Sabbath. Children, youth, and adults can all share what they have gleaned throughout the week.

In light of this, parents have a vital role to play in this Sabbath school work.

"Parents, set apart a little time each day for the study of the Sabbath-school lesson with your children." (*Testimonies on Sabbath School Work*, 10)

"The Sabbath-school affords to parents and children a precious opportunity for the study of God's Word. **But**

in order to gain that benefit which they should gain in the Sabbath-school, both parents and children should devote time to the study of the lessons, seeking to obtain a thorough knowledge of the facts presented, and also of the spiritual truths which these facts are designed to teach." (*Testimonies on Sabbath School Work*, 10, emphasis supplied)

4. Role of parents during class

Not only do parents have an important role throughout the week, but they also play an important role *during* class to help their children be engaged. Parents should remember that the purpose of the family Sabbath school is to help engage and interest their children in the study of the Bible. There should be no need to bring coloring books and activities for the children, as this is not the purpose of the Sabbath school.

To help keep their young children engaged, parents can, throughout the Sabbath school, quietly ask their children questions, such as, "Did you hear that question?" "What do you think about that?" "Oh, he's talking about and we were just talking about that this week." "Oh, listen, you know about that subject."

5. Parents, don't talk for your child.

Teachers can encourage children to speak and share, as well as encourage parents to allow their child to have the freedom to do so. Parents, allow your child to share his unfiltered, stuttering thoughts just as he wants to share them. When parents speak for their children, the children soon learn to not speak for themselves, which eventually leads them to not think for themselves either.

Chapter 9

Practical Points on the Structure and Function of the Family Bible-Study Sabbath School

1. A round-table format is best

In seeking to model our Sabbath School upon the Lord's plan, we must be careful to follow God's methods *completely*. Following only some of God's methods will not ensure success. One aspect of this change is that we must discard our traditional understanding of what it means to teach and to learn.

In the traditional educational environment, the teacher stands or sits at the front of the class and instructs the students who are seated in front of the teacher. This is so normal to us that even when adopting new methods of education we often retain this class arrangement, and we have applied it in the Sabbath school setting. This method has its roots in false education, especially in the Greek philosophy of education, in which the teacher is considered the "expert" and is to instruct the pupils and impart a certain set of information to them. Educational and brain research has shown us that this arrangement cultivates an attitude of passive receiving rather than active engagement.

Jesus did not teach by this method. He would gather the disciples around Him as He taught them. When the mothers brought their children to Jesus, he did not seat them in front of Him and instruct them. Rather, He gathered them around Him, allowing them to sit on His lap even. Notice the following description of how Jesus taught the disciples.

In the training of His disciples the Saviour followed the system of education established at the beginning. The Twelve first chosen, with a few others who through ministry to their needs were from time to time connected with them, formed the family of Jesus. They were with Him in the house, at the table, in the closet, in the field. They accompanied Him on His journeys, shared His trials and hardships, and, as much as in them was, entered into His work.

"Sometimes He taught them as they sat together on the mountainside, sometimes beside the sea, or from the fisherman's boat, sometimes as they walked by the way. Whenever He spoke to the multitude, the disciples formed the inner circle. They pressed close beside Him, that they might lose nothing of His instruction. They were attentive listeners, eager to understand the truths they were to teach in all lands and to all ages." (*Education*, 85)

We are told, "Christ's way of presenting truth cannot be improved upon." (Evangelism, 56) If we cannot improve upon Jesus' methods, should we not seek to emulate them as much as possible? We are instructed, "If ever it has been essential that we understand and follow right methods of teaching and follow the example of Christ, it is now." (*Evangelism*, 53)

We do not find Jesus copying the teaching methods of the rabbis nor the Greek teachers of the world. While He was the supreme authority on every topic which He taught, He did not merely give lectures to passively-receiving audiences. He often asked questions, and sought to awaken interest and engagement in the themes He taught. If Jesus taught this way, should not we erring mortals, who have everything to learn, follow the same method? We should do everything possible to encourage a willingness to learn and a spirit of active participation in the study of God's word. Speaking of the attitude of the teacher or parent toward the study of God's word, this inspired counsel puts in best:

"I will no longer stand so far above you. Let us climb together, and we will see what can be gained by a united study of the Scriptures. Christ is the One who imparts all knowledge. Let us work together in an earnest effort to learn from God how to understand the truths of His word, and how to place these truths before others in their beauty and simplicity. Let us study together....The Bible is your guidebook and my guidebook. By asking questions you may suggest ideas that are new to me. Various ways of expressing the truth we are studying will bring light into our class Light will shine upon us as in the meekness and lowliness of Christ we study together." (*Counsels to Parents, Teachers, and Students*, 436)

So, if we are not copying the methods of the world where the teacher stands or sits in front of the class and imparts information, what is a better alternative for the Sabbath School setting as we seek to copy the methods of Jesus? A round-table layout is ideal. A round-table format is far more conducive to engaged study and participation and allows for easy viewing of each individual as they speak.

Scientific research has shown clearly that the round-table format is far more effective than the traditional format where the teacher stands at the front of the class. Studies have found improved student learning; increased engagement in class discussion and higher levels of participation, especially from usually more passive students; more engagement in study and problem solving; increased conceptual understanding of the topics studied; better recall and retention of the lesson; improved student attitudes; better attendance; and improved teacher-student and student-student relationships. Consider this quote from the *Journal of Learning Spaces*.

"A classroom with seating affixed and directed toward a podium at the front of the room results in instructors spending more time in lecture and students demonstrating less active engagement. In contrast, roundtable seating arrangements lead to instructors and students engaging in more active learning activities, resulting in improved learning outcomes." ("Classroom Seating Arrangements", Yale.edu, citing Brooks, D. Christopher. "Space and consequences: The impact of different formal learning spaces on instructor and student behavior." *Journal of Learning Spaces* 1, no 2, (2012)

A round-table format provides a comfortable space for the usually-timid individual to engage in the discussion. It also provides a not-so-scary way for new or inexperienced teachers who may fear public speaking or getting in front of the class to lead out in the class study. Round-table formats promote the involvement of *everyone*.

A round-table format does not need to have an actual *table* - simply placing chairs in a circle is effective. However, if available, an actual table it does provide a comfortable place to put Bibles and study materials. If this is done, it is best to use a table that is actually *round*, or to arrange rectangular tables in the shape of a square, as research has found that a rectangular table is not ideal for promoting comfortable engagement and interaction from everyone. Some churches have a dedicated Sabbath school room and can put tables together for this format, while other churches often place chairs or a table at the front of the pews for the Sabbath school time. Priority for seats around the table should be given to families and young people, with overflow to the pews behind the table for additional people.

2. What lessons to use?

This is the Family *Bible-Study* Sabbath School class, and it is important to keep in mind that the focus is on the Bible and the stories of the Bible. It is not essential to use an actual lesson. One could just as easily use the Bible itself as the lesson, going through the stories in sequence. *The Conflict of the Ages* series is also an excellent guide. But for those who want a guide or for families who would like a structure to integrate the Sabbath school with their family worship, the *My Bible First* lessons provide an excellent format. There are varying levels, but for a wide-range of ages the *junior* lessons work well.

These lessons go through the Bible on a three-year cycle. They are adapted well to a wide-range of ages, as they have many Scripture references, and they suggest the correlated Spirit of Prophecy readings (primarily from the *Conflict of the Ages* series). These lessons also work well to integrate with family worship and could be read several times throughout the week with wonderful benefits and blessings.

Note: it is not necessary to follow the schedule of the lessons. Many classes take two or even three weeks to go through one lesson. What is most important is that the material is thoroughly understood and well learned by all.

3. Utilize the Spirit of Prophecy readings

The Spirit of Prophecy provides so much extra insight to the Bible stories and can add significant interest to the class. Parents and adults can use these readings throughout the week to enhance their own study and find insights and thoughts to share in class. The correlated Spirit of Prophecy readings are one of the great aspects of the *My Bible First* lessons.

4. Schedule a leader rotation

A leader rotation is important for maintaining interest. A schedule is helpful, and youth and older children should be included as class leaders.

5. Be flexible

An excellent method of teaching is to capitalize on the interest awakened.

"True education is not the forcing of instruction on an unready and unreceptive mind. The mental powers must be awakened, the interest aroused. For this, God's method of teaching provided. He who created the mind and ordained its laws, provided for its development in accordance with them. In the home and the sanctuary, through the things of nature and of art, in labor and in festivity, in sacred building and memorial stone, by methods and rites and symbols unnumbered, God gave to Israel lessons illustrating His principles and preserving the memory of His wonderful works. **Then, as inquiry was made, the instruction given impressed mind and heart**." (*Education*, 41, emphasis supplied)

When a question is asked that would make a valuable study point, especially regarding a key Bible teaching or doctrine, don't be afraid to take a break from the lessons to explore that topic. You never know when that interest will be piqued again.

Chapter 10

Common Questions or Objections

Is the Family Bible-Study Sabbath School format effective when there are children from families without religious instruction?

Sometimes children who attend the Sabbath school come from families that do not have family worship or religious instruction in the home. While ideally the family Sabbath school should be an extension and continuation of family worship, sadly this is not always the case since some families do not have family worship or even any form of religious instruction in the home.

First, it is important to realize that reaching these children is not necessarily the first purpose of Sabbath school. Certainly, it can be a tool for this, but it is not the only or the primary purpose.

"Even greater care should be taken by the parents to see that their children have their Scripture lessons than is taken to see that their day-school lessons are prepared. Their Scripture lessons should be learned more perfectly than their lessons in the common schools. *If parents and children see no necessity for this interest*, **then the children might better remain at home; for the Sabbath-school will fail to prove a blessing to them**." (*Testimonies on Sabbath School Work*, 7)

We see from this that even the best conducted Sabbath school will fail of its intended purpose if the children are not receiving spiritual instruction at home.

But must nothing be done to help reach these children? We should certainly make efforts to reach them, and the Sabbath school can also be a missionary endeavor.

"Parents who can be approached in no other way are frequently reached through their children. Sabbath-school teachers can instruct the children in the truth, and they will, in turn, take it into the home circle." (*Testimonies on Sabbath School Work*, 9)

So, although it is best that children have spiritual instruction in the home, we may still reach those who do not through the means of Sabbath school.

The point is this: family Sabbath school is best when it is an extension of what is happening at home, but it doesn't preclude those who don't have that advantage. They will be benefited by being a part of the *family* Sabbath school just as much, and probably more, than the traditional Sabbath school setting. When properly conducted, the Family Bible-Study Sabbath School will in many ways resemble family worship and thus provide these children with a taste of what they should be getting at home – as will the parents if they are in attendance. They will learn something in this environment, rather than just being entertained. Keep in mind it may require some flexibility and adaptation on the spot at times.

In cases where a large number of children are attending from families without religious instruction and these children may be a serious disruption and poor influence upon others, there are several steps and adaptations that should be taken.

First, educate parents upon the value of the family-oriented class, *encouraging them to attend Sabbath School with their children*. This may be a new concept to many, but is often readily accepted with sufficient explanation. The experience may prove to be life-changing.

Second, parents should be instructed in how to conduct family worship in their own homes. This can be done by the *example* of the Family Bible-study Sabbath School class. By observing and *participating* in the Sabbath school, parents can see and understand on a practical level how to carry out family worship in their home. Give parents practical tools and lesson assignments to do in their family worship during the week.

Third, keep the classes small. Ideally, two or three families are sufficient, with one family who understands and practices these principles and the other one or two families being the "missionary endeavor." Large classes become difficult to manage if there are unruly children.

Fourth, teachers must prepare *well*. Plan ahead with many methods to engage the class. Remember, your goal is engagement and interest, not entertainment. With the understanding that many in your class may have very short attention spans, come prepared with plenty of questions, examples, object lessons, etc. to keep everyone engaged in the study. Remember also that the study of God's word has power to transform and strengthen the mind, so expect, by prayer and God's grace, that your job will get easier as those who are unaccustomed to the study of the Bible become transformed by its power.

What about the very little children?

A common question regards the very little children. Will the little ones truly gain something from the family Sabbath school, or would it be better to wait until they are a few years old?

Remember the Biblical model. Even the suckling babes were to attend the religious services. Brain research tells us that children absorb far more than we realize. Even before they can talk, they understand most of what is said. The Lord knew this, and He instructed the parents to bring even their littlest ones to the religious services.

The best place for the little one is sitting on mom's lap. A child's relationship with mom is far more important than getting information into their mind. He/she can be content to sit on mom's lap, perhaps with a favorite blanket or object to handle, and mom can make efforts to speak to the child about what is said and done throughout the class. (Refer to the role of parents during class from chapter 7.) This teaches the little one that this class is something that he is to learn to engage in. The child will absorb what he/she hears and, if the class is being conducted well to engage the children, you'll be surprised one day when the little one voices a thought about something and you realize he/she were listening all the time.

Doesn't the Spirit of Prophecy encourage age-segregated Sabbath schools?

A common objection to the concept of the age-integrated class, is the perception that the Spirit of Prophecy encourages age-segregated Sabbath schools. A superficial reading of the Spirit of Prophecy may appear to indicate that age segregation was the recommendation, but deeper study reveals the opposite.

It is important to realize that when the counsel on Sabbath school was given, the Sunday schools of the day (which Sabbath schools modeled in many respects) were an entity that in many aspects functioned independently of the church services, and were modeled after the traditional school setting in many ways. They were entirely focused on the children, and many children – even children from completely irreligious backgrounds – attended Sunday school completely independent of their parents (just like regular school).

The counsel in the Spirit of Prophecy regarding Sabbath school work was actually seeking to elevate the norm of the day to include the parents and get the whole family involved. This was a challenge to the norm of the day and would have been quite a change for many parents. Perhaps the suggestion of a family Sabbath school would have been too radical for the time, but encouragement is definitely given to include the parents, which would have been a rather surprising statement at the time.

"There should be cooperation on the part of parent, children, and teachers." (*Testimonies on Sabbath School Work*, 20)

"Parents should search the Scriptures with their children. They should become familiar with the lessons themselves; then they can assist their children in learning them. Every day some portion of time should be appropriated to the study of the lessons, not merely in learning to mechanically repeat the words, while the mind does not comprehend the meaning; but to go to the very foundation, and become familiar with what is brought out in the lesson. The indifference of the children, in very many cases, is chargeable to the parents. They are indifferent, and the children catch the same spirit. If parents show that they attach importance to the Sabbath school, by giving it respect and prominence, the children will generally copy their example." (*Counsels on Sabbath School Work*, 53)

It is also important to recognize that the Spirit of Prophecy does not describe *exactly* how the Sabbath school should be set up and function. Many principles are given, but the counsel does not limit the structure and function to a certain method. Rather, it encourages growth and improvement, with a constant reminder that the parents must be involved.

"Our Sabbath-schools are nothing less than Bible societies, and in the sacred work of teaching the truths of God's Word, they can accomplish far more than they have hitherto accomplished. The Sabbath- school, when rightly managed, possesses marvelous power, and is adapted to doing a great work, but it is not now what it may and should be." (*Testimonies on Sabbath School Work*, 29)

"I have been shown that you should have less burden of form, and a greater burden to see deep heart work in the Sabbath-school....Teachers will become disqualified for their position if they are not learners. They need freshness of ideas, fresh, wise plans, life, tact, and spirit in their work." (Testimonies on Sabbath School Work, 24)

And in some places the Spirit of Prophecy does actually recommend the gathering of all ages.

"Gather the **infants with lisping lips, the youth and the aged**, and set them to the task of solving mysteries which have not been comprehended by the wise men of earth, although possessed of giant minds." (*Testimonies on Sabbath School Work*, 31, emphasis supplied)

Chapter 11

Ready to Start!

The Family Bible-Study Sabbath School class has so many benefits, but how to actually get started?

The specifics of how to start will depend greatly upon the church.

For large- and medium-sized churches, you'll want to go through the appropriate channels for starting a new Sabbath school class. Perhaps there is another family or two that you can start it with. A simple, "This is a new Sabbath school class with an exciting format. It's for the entire family. All ages are encouraged to attend, and we will be studying through the Bible. All are welcome!" is usually sufficient "advertising". As curiosity motivates people to check out the new class, many will stay because they enjoy it and see the value.

For small churches, the family Bible-study class is especially beneficial as it eliminates the need to have several classes (typically with only a handful of students) and unites the entire church in a single class for the study of God's word. It is usually best to propose that you have an idea that you would like the church to consider. Prepare a short presentation and explain the benefits and scriptural basis for the model, and suggest that you would like to give the idea a try for a trial period – perhaps for a few months or a quarter. Most people will be willing to give the idea a try and usually greatly enjoy the class and want to continue.

To get started, keep it simple. Gather your family and the others who want to join around a table (even if it's only two families), and open your Bibles. Pick a story, or start with Genesis or the gospels, and take turns reading. Encourage all to be engaged. Ask questions, and find answers in the Word of God. Use a lesson guide if you wish, and organize a schedule of study and leadership. Study the topic more in family worship throughout the week, and all – young and old alike – will have something to share. All will find joy in the study of the Bible.

The Family Bible-Study Sabbath School model may seem like a new idea, but it is simply a revival and returning to the simple methods the Lord has given in His Word. We would do well to follow His ways, trusting that He who knows best the developing mind can be trusted to provide the best methods of instruction.

If you're not quite sure of all the details of how to go about it, give it a try! The Lord will guide and make your way plain as you seek to win the souls of our precious children.

Chapter 12

Success Stories

These stories are true. Names have been changed.

A dead church:

Smithville church was dead. There were no young people or children left. Just a handful of the older members came each Sabbath, and the conference was planning to close the church. That could have been the end of the story, as it has been for many other churches, but, thankfully, it wasn't. Rob and his family, who were members of a nearby church, offered to make a last-ditch effort to resurrect Smithville. It would take something new and creative, as all the usual strategies had been tried to no avail. A radical plan was needed.

Rob turned to the Bible. With his four children and one other family, he began a weekly Bible study at the Smithville church focused on the children. They began with basic Bible doctrines.

"At first the older members objected to not having the usual adult-Sabbath-School-Quarterly study," Rob says. "But I sold the idea on the fact that we were helping the children. Besides, they were ready to try anything to avoid shutting the church down. We had nothing to lose."

Rob was careful to keep the lessons simple and Bible-based. He focused on maintaining an interactive format that kept the children involved. "It was nothing complicated," Rob explains, "but we found the simple Bible lessons taught in an interactive way were intensely interesting to the children – and their parents." As they worked through the Bible doctrines week after week, interest grew. Visitors started showing up. Families from other churches started coming. Community children started coming and bringing their parents.

Rob continues, "The adults were actually enjoying the studies as much as the children. We began to realize that the parents needed as much instruction in these basic Bible doctrines as the children did!"

The program was a hit. By the time Rob finished with the Bible doctrines and began a study of the sanctuary, the church was getting full. Now in their third year and working through the book of Revelation (with the children!), families are travelling from up to two hours away just to attend the Sabbath school program! "We want our children to have this instruction," parents say, "not to mention that we need it too."

Smithville church is now far from dead. It is a vibrant church, full of youth and children, with over seventy-five people attending every Sabbath morning.

God's simple methods will always bring success and only await our trusting obedience.

A large church:

Jonesville church was an active church with good attendance, but a few parents were concerned about the influences of peer-associations in the age-segregated classes. "I wished we could study together," one of them explained. "I wanted a Sabbath-school program that would draw us together as a family and that would connect better with our family worships throughout the week."

Finding abundant Biblical evidence in favor of a family-based class, two of the families decided to have a simple study together during the Sabbath school time. They didn't have any lessons available, so they made their own, working their way through basic Bible doctrines, a study of the sanctuary, and the Protestant Reformation. The class was open for anyone to attend, although it was encouraged that the entire family attend together.

It was a simple start, but the large fellowship hall where the class was held was soon bursting at its seams. "We had no idea there would be so much interest in the class," the parents said. "It seems this has scratched an itch!" Families came with their little ones, youth came on their own, and all fell in love with the simple Bible study which satisfied their spiritual hunger.

"It was such an encouragement to me to just simply follow God's methods," a parent said. "They will bring true success."

A small church:

The Georgetown church was a small church, attended by a few earnest families. The church was conservative-minded, present-truth focused, and family-oriented, but, despite all these good things, the youth didn't seem to be following in the footsteps of their parents. The younger generation lacked spiritual strength. "As difficult as it was to face, we realized that we were slowly losing our youth," one of the parents explained. "They were coming to church every week but, in reality, lacked a relationship with God. They seemed uninterested in spiritual things and rarely engaged in discussion – even in the youth class."

Church leadership and parents were pulling their hair out to come up with methods to get the youth more engaged – youth class, youth-led studies, and youth events – but nothing seemed to work. But when someone proposed the idea of a family Bible study class, it met with significant opposition. "If they're not engaged in the youth class, how will they be engaged in a Bible study class with adults?" some argued. Others objected, "Our adult class is just going to become a children's class. We need real spiritual food, not the children's lessons!"

The age-segregated classes at such a small church meant sparse attendance in each class and a lot of work for the few leaders, and those proposing the family class would have preferred the entire church to unite in the endeavor. But with such opposition, the three families who wanted to try the idea decided there was no need to try to convince everyone. "We just simply gathered our three families together and gave it a try," they said.

Four Sabbaths later, there was only one couple with no children remaining in the adult class. Everyone who visited the family Bible-study class wanted to stay. The couple remaining in the adult class acquiesced and found themselves enjoying the class too. Soon, the class was so popular that people started coming for the Sabbath school class instead of church!

And the youth? "It was like you flipped a switch," one parent said. "I've never seen my young people so interested and engaged. I've seen spiritual growth in my young people that I would never have imagined. The round-table format was absolutely important key." The youth started studying on their own and bringing their thoughts to class. Some started leading out in the class. The church retained their youth and was a vibrant active church for the several years that they kept the Family Bible-study Sabbath School class.

www.ingramcontent.com/pod-product-compliance
Lightning Source LLC
Chambersburg PA
CBHW071908020426

42331CB00010B/2719